ADDITION FACTS THAT STICK

ADDITION FACTS THAT STICK

Help Your Child Master the Addition Facts
for Good in Just Six Weeks

KATE SNOW

WELL-TRAINED MIND PRESS

TABLE OF CONTENTS

WEEK 1: ADDING ONE AND TWO / 17

WEEK 2: PAIRS THAT MAKE TEN / 25

WEEK 3: SUMS LESS THAN TEN / 31

WEEK 4: ADDING NINE / 37

PREFACE

My first job out of college was teaching fifth grade in an excellent public school in the Boston suburbs. I was thrilled to have the chance to work in such a great school district, and I could hardly wait to meet my students as I prepared for my first year of teaching.

Most of all, I was excited to teach math. I majored in math in college, and I eagerly looked forward to sharing my love of the subject with my students. Even before school began, I started to plan lessons covering the usual fifth-grade topics, like geometry, fractions, decimals, and percentages.

However, it only took a couple weeks of school for me to realize that some of my students needed a better mastery of the basics—especially the addition facts—before they'd be ready to tackle fifth-grade work. My colleagues in the lower grades assured me that they'd taught the addition facts diligently and encouraged parents to work on the facts at home. So why did I have bright ten-year-olds in my class who couldn't add eight plus five?

As I probed further, I discovered that nearly all of my students had once memorized the addition facts. But the facts just hadn't stuck. Their teachers and parents had con-scientiously made flash cards and drilled the flash cards over and over. This method had worked for some of the children. But for others, it seemed that the addition facts had gone straight into their short-term memories and then straight out again.

So, instead of repeating a method that hadn't worked, I decided to try a different approach with my fifth-grade students. Instead of using rote memorization to master the addition facts, I taught my students how to visualize the numbers and use mental strategies to find the solutions. This took a little teaching time at the beginning, but the results were worth it. At first, it took my students a few seconds to apply the strategies when finding sums. But with a little practice, the strategies became so automatic that they "just knew" the answers. I'm proud to say that every student in my class had fully mastered the addition facts before Thanksgiving—and had become much more confi-dent and successful in their math studies as a result.

That was nearly fifteen years ago. Since then, I've taught several years of fifth-grade math classes, written math curricula, tutored students who struggle in math, and begun homeschooling my own children. Through these experiences, I've refined the approach I used with my first class of fifth-graders to create a simple, effective program that will help any child master the addition facts—all without flash cards or rote memorization.

Over the years, I've met so many parents who want to help their children master these important math foundations but just aren't sure how to do so effectively. That's why I've written this book. It will guide you step by step as you help your child master the addition facts, once and for all, so that the addition facts truly stick.

INTRODUCTION

What makes this approach unique?

~~Practice all the addition facts at once.~~

Target one small group of addition facts at a time.

Instead of overwhelming your child with all 81 addition facts, this program breaks the addition facts into smaller groups. The facts in each group can be solved with the same strategy. So, instead of memorizing each fact individually, your child can learn one strategy and then apply the strategy to the entire group. It's a lot simpler to learn six strategies than it is to memorize 81 different facts.

~~Memorize answers.~~

Visualize numbers and use strategies to find the answers.

When children think about numbers, they tend to visualize piles of disorganized counters. So, to add 8 + 4, they imagine a pile of eight counters and a pile of four counters and then count them all up to find the sum.

How most children imagine 8 + 4.

But since counting is slow, inefficient, and error-prone, many parents resort to having their children memorize the addition facts by rote instead. In this book, rather than teaching your child to memorize each fact individually, you'll use a simple grid of ten squares (called a ten-frame) to help your child visualize the numbers up to ten.

The ten-frame, a simple tool for helping visualize numbers.

When children learn to visualize numbers on a ten-frame, they can use simple strategies to break numbers apart and put them together efficiently and accurately. For example, to add 8 + 4, your child will learn to imagine both numbers on ten-frames.

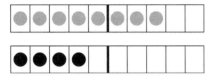

8 + 4 modeled on the ten-frame. Notice how much easier it is to tell how many counters are in each row without counting each one by one.

Then, your child can simply visualize moving two counters to the top row to complete the row. Now, it's easy to see that the answer is 10 + 2, or 12.

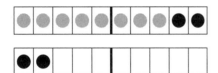

Moving two counters to the top row makes it easy to see that 8 + 4 = 12.

With just six simple strategies like this one, your child will know all of the addition facts.

~~Drill the flash cards over and over.~~

Practice applying strategies to increase speed.

Instead of drilling flash cards over and over so that your child is exposed to the right answer enough times to memorize it, your child will practice *using strategies* until they become automatic. With consistent practice at applying the six strategies, your child will get faster and faster at figuring out the answers—and before long, he or she will "just know" the answers and have them fully mastered.

~~**Review flash cards constantly to prevent forgetting.**~~

Teach addition facts that stick!

When children memorize the addition facts individually, it's very easy to forget them, so constant review is necessary. But when children who have learned addition fact *strategies* momentarily forget a fact, they can figure out the correct answer quickly and easily—without any additional drill.

HOW TO USE THIS BOOK

This program is divided into six units, each designed to take about a week. Each unit targets a small group of addition facts that can be solved with the same mental strategy. You'll follow the same pattern of activities each week. By the end of six weeks, your child will have learned all the addition facts.

You'll use three different activities each week to help your child master the focus facts for the week: direct teaching, games, and written practice.

Day 1: Introduce new facts and teach a new game

On the first day of each week, you will use counters and a ten-frame to help your child learn to visualize numbers. You'll explain the new mental strategy to your child and ask questions to make sure he or she understands it. (Don't worry if you have never taught math before—this book will guide you step by step.)

Next, you will teach your child a game that provides lots of practice with the focus facts for the week. The games are not only fun, but they also provide a lot of practice in a short amount of time. Even more importantly, they allow you to quickly correct any mistakes and monitor how well your child is using the new mental strategy.

Days 2–5: Play game and complete practice pages

For the rest of the week, you will play the new game again each day. As you play, you'll encourage your child to continue using the mental strategy introduced on Day 1.

Your child will also complete a short practice page each day. This will give your child practice at solving the week's addition facts in written form. The practice pages also review all the addition facts your child has learned in previous weeks.

Teaching tips

- Schedule a consistent time each day for addition fact practice. You'll be less likely to forget, and your child will be less likely to argue. Try to choose a time when your child is alert and easily able to concentrate.
- Plan to work on the activities in this book for about 15 minutes each session, with five sessions per week. However, different children need different amounts of time to master each strategy. Feel free to take more than five days with each strategy if needed.
- Discourage your child from counting to solve problems. For example, many first- or second-graders might solve 8 + 5 by starting at eight and counting on five more: "8...9...10...11...12...13. The answer is 13." However, counting is extremely inefficient and error-prone. Think how many opportunities there are to make a mistake if you use counting to find 9 + 8! The only exception to this is Week 1, when your child will count forward one or two to solve the +1 and +2 facts. There are a lot fewer chances for errors when you're only adding on one or two.
- Keep the practice sessions positive, upbeat, and fast-paced. Have fun playing the games with your child, and enjoy the one-on-one time together.
- If you child is a reluctant writer, don't let writing difficulties interfere with mastering the addition facts. It's fine to have your child answer the worksheet problems orally rather than writing them.
- Many young children freeze when they feel time pressure. Unless your child is age ten or older, don't time him or her on the practice pages. For an older child, aim for your child to know each addition fact in three seconds or less.

Is your child ready to master the addition facts?

This book is designed for children who have had some exposure to numbers and addition but do not yet know the answers to the addition facts automatically. While it's fine to introduce your younger child to the games and strategies, don't expect thorough mastery of the addition facts until your child is *at least* six years old.

To be successful at mastering the addition facts, your child should first:

- Be able to count to 20 and recognize written numbers up to 20
- Understand that addition means putting two parts together to make a whole, and that numbers can be added in any order without changing the sum (i.e., that 3 + 2 = 2 + 3)
- Have a beginning understanding of place-value (for example, knowing that 15 is the same as 10 + 5)

If your child has these foundational skills in place, he or she is ready to master the addition facts.

What you'll need

All of the game boards and practice pages you'll need for this program are included in the back of the book. You'll also need a few everyday items to complete the activities and play the games:

- 15 small counters of two different colors (coins, dry beans, buttons, blocks, etc.)
- Coin (any kind)
- Two game tokens
- Paper and pencil
- Two decks of regular playing cards

WEEK 1

ADDING ONE AND TWO

WEEK 1 AT A GLANCE

Strategy: Count forward from the larger number.

This week, your child will learn to add one or two to single-digit numbers by counting forward from the larger addend. For example, to solve 6 + 2, he'll count "6, 7, 8."

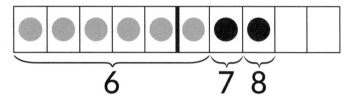

Counting forward from 6 to find 6 + 2.

He'll also learn to recognize quantities on the ten-frame, which will prepare him to master more difficult addition facts in later weeks. Even if your child already knows the +1 and +2 addition facts, don't skip this week's ten-frame activities—it is important for him to become familiar with this extremely useful way of visualizing numbers.

This week, your child will learn these new facts:

1 + 1 = 2	2 + 2 = 4
2 + 1 = 3	3 + 2 = 5
3 + 1 = 4	4 + 2 = 6
4 + 1 = 5	5 + 2 = 7
5 + 1 = 6	6 + 2 = 8
6 + 1 = 7	7 + 2 = 9
7 + 1 = 8	8 + 2 = 10
8 + 1 = 9	(9 + 2 = 11 will be covered in Week 4.)
9 + 1 = 10	

You will need:

- Ten-frames (page 57)
- Coin
- 15 small counters of two different colors
- Week 1 Practice Pages (pages 77–83)

DAY 1: NEW TEACHING

Introduce the ten-frame

Show your child the ten-frames. Draw his attention to the top ten-frame.

"How many boxes are to the left of the dark line?" *Five.*
"How many boxes are to the right of the dark line?" *Five.*
"How many boxes are in this entire frame?" *Ten.*
Place six counters on the ten-frame.

"How many counters are there?" *Six.*
If your child counts each counter individually, say, "There's a shortcut for finding the number of counters without counting each one. How many counters are to the left of the dark line?" *Five.*
"How many counters are to the right of the dark line?" *One.*
"So, there's one counter more than five. What's one more than five?" *Six.*
"Let's try another one." Place nine counters on the ten-frame.

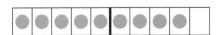

"How many counters are there?" *Nine.*

If your child counts each counter individually, show him that he can think of the five counters on the left-hand side as a group and then count forward from five for each additional counter.

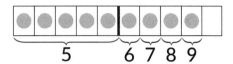

Your child will get more practice at recognizing quantities on the ten-frame in this week's game.

Introduce +1 facts

Place six counters on the ten-frame again.

"If I add one counter to the ten-frame, then how many counters will there be?" *Seven.*

Have your child place one counter of a different color on the ten-frame to check his answer (or to find the answer, if he's not sure). Point out that he doesn't need to count each counter one by one to figure out how many there are. Since there were already six counters, he can just count forward one from six ("6, 7") to find the new number of counters.

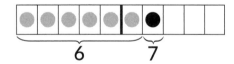

Write **6 + 1 =** on a sheet of paper.

"There were six counters (point to the 6), and then I added one more (point to the plus sign and 1). So, since six counters plus one counter equals seven counters, six plus one equals seven." Complete the written addition problem: **6 + 1 = 7**.

Introduce +2 facts

Write **7 + 2** = on a piece of paper. Have your child help you represent the problem by placing seven counters on the ten-frame and then adding two counters of a different color.

"How many counters are on the ten-frame now?" *Nine.* If needed, encourage him to count forward from seven to find the answer: "7, 8, 9."

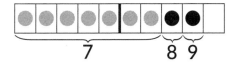

"So, what's seven plus two?" *Nine.* Have your child complete the written problem: **7 + 2 = 9**.

Have your child use counters to model the other addition facts for this week and find their answers. (They are listed on the previous page.) Make sure he always starts with the larger number on the ten-frame and fills in the ten-frame from left to right without skipping any boxes. This makes it easier to "see" the answers and count forward from the larger number.

Adding numbers in any order

Write **2 + 7 =** on a piece of paper.

Have your child represent this problem by placing two counters on the ten-frame and then adding seven counters of a different color.

"How many counters are on the ten-frame now?" *Nine.*

"So, what's two plus seven?" *Nine.* Have your child complete the written addition problem: **2 + 7 = 9**.

"That's the same answer that we got for 7 + 2. We can add numbers in any order and still get the same answer."

"Adding is usually easier when you start with the bigger number and then add on the smaller number, no matter what order the numbers are written in."

To give your child practice with starting with the bigger number, write **2 + 5 =** on a piece of paper. Have your child solve the problem by first placing five counters on the ten-frame and then adding two more to find that the answer is seven. Have him complete the written problem: **2 + 5 = 7**.

Play *Race to Ten*

Teach your child to play *Race to Ten* and play several times.

MATERIALS

- Ten-frames (page 57)
- Coin
- 20 small counters

OBJECT OF THE GAME

Be the first to reach ten.

HOW TO PLAY

Each player chooses one ten-frame to fill.

On your turn, flip the coin. If it is heads, add one counter to your ten-frame. If it is tails, add two counters to your ten-frame. Say the matching addition fact as you place the counters. For example, if you had four counters on your ten-frame and then added two, you would say, "Four plus two equals six."

Then, it is the other player's turn. Continue until one person has filled his whole ten-frame. Keep the game fun and fast-paced.

GAME NOTE

Always fill in the ten-frame in order, from left to right. Encourage your child to count up from the larger number to figure out the number of counters on the ten-frame.

DAYS 2–5: *RACE TO TEN* AND PRACTICE PAGES

Each day, play *Race to Ten* several times.

Also have your child complete one Week 1 Practice Page each day. If he gets stuck, encourage him to count up from the larger addend, using counters on the ten-frame as needed. Answers to the Practice Pages can be found on page 126.

WEEK 2

PAIRS THAT
MAKE TEN

WEEK 2 AT A GLANCE

Strategy: Visualize full and empty boxes on the ten-frame.

This week, your child will learn the pairs of numbers that sum to ten. She'll master these facts by visualizing full and empty boxes on the ten-frame. For example, if seven boxes on the ten-frame are full, three are empty, so $7 + 3 = 10$.

Seven boxes are full, and three boxes are empty. So, 7 + 3 = 10.

There are only five of these facts, but they are essential building blocks for mastering the rest of the addition facts. (Your child learned $9 + 1$ and $8 + 2$ last week, but she will review them this week in the context of full and empty boxes on the ten-frame.)

This week, your child will learn these new facts:

$5 + 5 = 10$
$6 + 4 = 10$
$7 + 3 = 10$
$8 + 2 = 10$
$9 + 1 = 10$

You will need:

- Ten-frames (page 57)
- Ten-frame cards 1–9 (page 59), cut apart on the dotted lines
- Paper and pencil
- Ten small counters
- Extra piece of blank paper
- Deck of cards, with face cards removed
- Week 2 Practice Pages (pages 85–91)

DAY 1: NEW TEACHING

Warm-up activity

Show your child the ten-frame card for six.

"How many boxes are full?" *Six.* Point out that the dark line in the middle divides the ten-frame into groups of five. So, there are five boxes full on the left side of the frame, plus one more box, for a total of six boxes.

Discuss a couple more cards in this way to make sure your child understands what the cards show.

Shuffle all of the ten-frame cards. Flash each card for a second or two and ask how many boxes are full. Adjust your pace to your child, and stop and allow more time to look at a card if needed. Encourage your child to use reasoning—not counting one by one—to figure out how many boxes are full on each card.

Introduce new facts

Place seven counters on the ten-frame.

"How many boxes are full? How many are empty?" *Seven are full. Three are empty.* "So, what must seven plus three equal?" *Ten, since the ten-frame has ten boxes.*

If your child isn't sure, explain that the ten-frame has ten boxes. So, if seven full boxes and three empty boxes fill the ten-frame, the two numbers added together must equal ten.

Write **7 + 3 = 10** on a sheet of paper.

Repeat for the other addition facts for this week, as shown below. Always start with the larger number on the ten-frame so that it is easier to "see" how many empty boxes there are without counting.

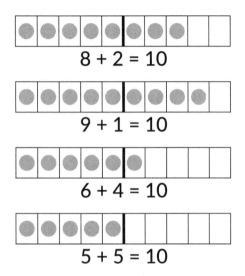

Practice visualizing combinations

Secretly put eight counters on the ten-frame.

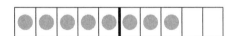

Cover the ten-frame with a sheet of paper.

"I'm going to let you see the counters for just a second. Your job is to figure out how many boxes are full and how many are empty."

Take away the paper for two seconds. Then cover the ten-frame again. "How many boxes are full? How many are empty?" *Eight are full, with two boxes empty.*

If your child is not sure, uncover the ten-frame. Let her look for a longer period of time and count if necessary. The main goal is for her to start to visualize what ten looks like and how ten can be partitioned into two groups.

Repeat this activity with seven, six, nine, and five counters on the mat. As your child gets better at determining how many boxes are full and empty, uncover the mat for shorter and shorter periods of time.

Play *Tens Go Fish*

Teach your child how to play *Tens Go Fish* and play several times.

MATERIALS

- Deck of cards, with tens and face cards removed

OBJECT OF THE GAME

Collect the most pairs that equal ten.

HOW TO PLAY

This game is just like regular *Go Fish*, but with a twist. Instead of matching pairs with the same number, match pairs whose sum is ten.

Shuffle the cards. Deal five cards to each player. Leave the rest face down in the middle of the table as the "fish pond."

On your turn, ask for a card that would create a sum of ten with a card already in your hand. (For example, if you have a six, ask for a four.) Your opponent must give you the card if she has it. If she doesn't have the card, she says, "Go fish!" and you take a card from the fish pond. If you get a pair, place it face-up in front of you and say the corresponding addition fact.

Play until all the cards are used up. Players who run out of cards before the fish pond is used up may take two cards from the fish pond to continue playing. Whoever has more pairs at the end of the game is the winner.

GAME NOTE

If your child is having trouble figuring out what card to ask for, have her build a number from her cards on a ten-frame and look to see how many empty squares are left.

DAYS 2–5: *TENS GO FISH AND PRACTICE PAGES*

Each day, play *Tens Go Fish* several times. Then, have your child complete one Week 2 Practice Page. If she gets stuck, encourage her to visualize the ten-frame or physically place counters on it to represent the problem.

Answers to this week's Practice Pages are on page 127.

WEEK 3

SUMS LESS THAN TEN

WEEK 3 AT A GLANCE

Strategy: Use five as a reference point.

This week, your child will tackle the last few sums less than ten. Each of these sums contains a number close to five, so your child will use the dividing line in the middle of the ten-frame as a mental reference point. For example, to solve 4 + 3, your child will first add one to the four to make a five, and then add the remaining two.

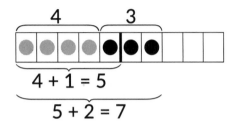

Using the dividing line as a reference point to break 4 + 3 into two problems that are easier to visualize: 4 + 1 = 5 and 5 + 2 = 7.

This week, your child will learn these new facts:

4 + 3 = 7
4 + 4 = 8
5 + 4 = 9
5 + 3 = 8
6 + 3 = 9
3 + 3 = 6

You will need:

- Ten-frames (page 57)
- Paper and pencil
- 15 small counters of two different colors (30 total)
- Extra piece of blank paper
- Two *Climb to the Top* game boards (one for each player, pages 61 and 63)
- Threes, fours, fives, and sixes from a deck of cards (four of each, 16 total cards)
- Week 3 Practice Pages (pages 93–99)

DAY 1: NEW TEACHING

Introduce new facts

Write **4 + 3 =** on a piece of paper and place four counters on the ten-frame.

"Imagine if I added three counters. First, I'd use one counter to fill in the empty box to complete the group of five." (Point to this box.)

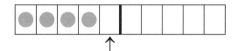

"Then, I'd still need to add two more counters on the other side of the dark line." (Point to these two boxes.)

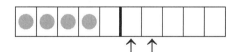

"How many counters would there be then?" *Seven.*

Have your child physically place three counters of a different color on the ten-frame to confirm the answer.

Have your child complete the written addition problem: **4 + 3 = 7**.

Repeat with the other addition facts for this week, as shown below. Always start with the larger number on the ten-frame, and ask your child to visualize the second number in the problem *before* constructing it with counters. As in the example above, remind him to use the dark line in the middle of the ten-frame as a visual anchor to help him "see" the answers rather than counting each counter one by one.

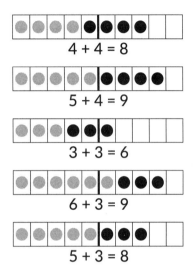

Practice visualizing combinations

Secretly put four counters of one color and three counters of the other color on the ten-frame. Cover the mat with a sheet of paper.

"I'm going to uncover the ten-frame for just a second. Your job is to tell me what addition problem the counters show."

Take away the paper for two seconds, then cover the mat again. "What addition problem does this show?" (4 + 3 = 7, or 3 + 4 = 7.)

If he's not sure, uncover the mat and let him look for a longer period of time and count if necessary.

Repeat with the other addition facts from the previous activity (4 + 4 = 8, 5 + 4 = 9, 6 + 3 = 9, 3 + 3 = 6). As your child gets better at recognizing the combinations, uncover the mat for shorter and shorter periods of time.

Play *Climb to the Top*

Teach your child how to play *Climb to the Top* and play several times.

MATERIALS

- Two *Climb to the Top* game boards (pages 61–63)

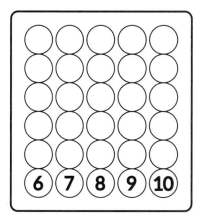

- Threes, fours, fives, and sixes from a deck of cards (four cards of each kind; 16 cards total)
- 15 small counters per player

OBJECT OF THE GAME

Be the first player to fill in an entire column and reach the top of the game board.

HOW TO PLAY

Shuffle the cards and place the stack face down on the table. On your turn, turn over the top two cards and find the sum of the cards. Place a counter on the lowest empty box in the column that matches the sum. For example, if you draw a five and a three, place a counter in the box above the eight. Sums greater than ten are wild, and you get to choose which column to place the counter in.

Play then passes to the other player. Continue until one player has filled in an entire column and reached the top.

As you play, continue to encourage your child to visualize the sums on the ten-frame rather than construct them with counters, but allow him to construct them if needed.

DAYS 2–5: *CLIMB TO THE TOP AND PRACTICE PAGES*

Each day, play *Climb to the Top* several times. Then, have your child complete one Week 3 Practice Page to practice writing the answers to this week's addition facts and to review facts learned so far. If he gets stuck, encourage him to either visualize the numbers on the ten-frame or physically put counters on the ten-frame. As in Week 1, remind him to always begin with the larger number in each problem to make it easier to use the middle line of the ten-frame as a reference point. (For example, when solving 3 + 6, have him first put six counters on the ten-frame and then add three more.)

Answers to this week's Practice Pages are on page 128.

WEEK 4

ADDING NINE

WEEK 4 AT A GLANCE

Strategy: Make a group of ten.

Now that your child has learned all of the sums up to ten, it's time to tackle the sums greater than ten. This week, she will learn all of the +9 addition facts. Now that the sums are greater than ten, she will use two ten-frames to model the problems. For example, here is how she will represent 9 + 4.

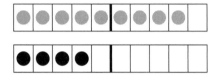

9 + 4 modeled on the ten-frames.

To solve these problems, she will move one counter from the bottom ten-frame to the top ten-frame to make a complete group of ten on the top ten-frame.

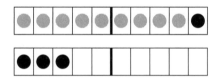

Moving one counter makes it easier to see that 9 + 4 = 13.

Once she moves the counter, she can use her knowledge of place-value to "see" the answer: Since there are ten counters on the top ten-frame and three counters on the bottom ten-frame, the answer is 13.

This week, your child will learn these new facts:

9 + 2 = 11	9 + 6 = 15
9 + 3 = 12	9 + 7 = 16
9 + 4 = 13	9 + 8 = 17
9 + 5 = 14	9 + 9 = 18

You will need:

- Ten-frames (page 57)
- Ten-frame cards 10–18 (page 65), cut apart on the dotted lines
- 15 counters of two different colors (30 counters total)
- Two *Adding Nines Bingo* game boards (one for each player, pages 67 and 69)
- Deck of cards, with tens and face cards removed
- Week 4 Practice Pages (pages 101–107)

DAY 1: NEW TEACHING

Warm-up activity

Show your child the ten-frame card for 14.

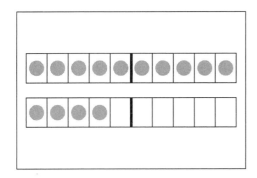

"How many boxes are full?" *14.* If she's not sure, point out that an entire row of ten is full, plus four more boxes. Encourage her to try to recognize the quantities rather than counting each full box one by one.

Discuss a couple more cards in this way to make sure your child understands what the cards show.

Shuffle all of the ten-frame cards. Flash each card for a second or two and ask how many boxes are full. Adjust your pace to your child, and stop and allow more time to look at a card if needed.

Introduce new facts

Write **9 + 4 =** on a piece of paper. Have your child help you model the problem with counters: Place nine counters of one color on the top ten-frame and four counters of another color on the bottom ten-frame.

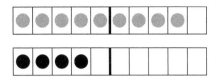

"To make it easier to figure out the answer, let's move a counter from the bottom row to the top row." Move one counter as shown.

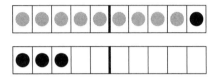

"How many counters are in the top row now?" *Ten.*

"How many counters are in the bottom row now?" *Three.*

"So, to solve nine plus four, you can add ten plus three instead. So, what's nine plus four?" *13.*

Have your child complete the written addition problem: **9 + 4 = 13**.

Repeat this process with the other +9 addition combinations (9 + 2, 9 + 3, 9 + 5, 9 + 6, 9 + 7, 9 + 8, 9 + 9). Have your child physically move a counter from the bottom ten-frame to the top ten-frame each time to complete the row of ten and make each problem easier to solve.

Play *Adding Nines Bingo*

Teach your child how to play *Adding Nines Bingo* and play several times.

MATERIALS

- Two *Adding Nines Bingo* game boards (One for each player, pages 67 and 69)

16	12	15	13	18
17	18	13	14	12
13	14	FREE	12	15
15	11	16	10	14
10	13	11	16	17

14	10	13	17	15
11	18	12	14	13
18	15	FREE	11	10
16	11	15	12	17
13	14	17	16	12

- Deck of cards, with tens and face cards removed (36 cards total)
- 15 small counters per player

OBJECT OF THE GAME

Be the first player to fill the boxes in an entire column, row, or diagonal.

HOW TO PLAY

This game is like traditional Bingo, with your child as the "caller."

To play, shuffle the cards and place them face down in a pile. Have your child turn over the top card and say the sum of the card plus nine. For example, if the card is a six, your child says, "Nine plus six equals 15."

Then, each of you uses a counter to cover a square containing the sum. (In the example, you would cover a square with a 15.) Continue until one of you wins by filling an entire column, row, or diagonal.

As you play, continue to encourage your child to visualize the sums on the ten-frame rather than construct them with counters, but allow her to construct them if needed.

DAYS 2–5: ADDING NINES BINGO AND PRACTICE PAGES

Each day, play *Adding Nines Bingo* several times. Then, have your child complete one Week 4 Practice Page to practice writing the answers to this week's addition facts and to review facts learned so far. If she gets stuck, encourage her to visualize the numbers on the ten-frame or physically represent the numbers with counters.

Answers to this week's Practice Pages are on page 129.

WEEK 5

ADDING EIGHT

WEEK 5 AT A GLANCE

Strategy: Make a group of ten.

Like last week, your child will use the "make ten" strategy as he learns the +8 addition facts this week. For example to solve 8 + 4, he'll first model the problem with counters.

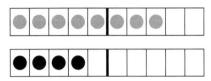

8 + 4 modeled on the ten-frames.

Then, he'll move two counters from the bottom ten-frame to the top ten-frame to make a complete group of ten on the top ten-frame. He'll again use his knowledge of place-value to "see" the answer: There are ten counters on the top and two counters on the bottom, so the answer is 12.

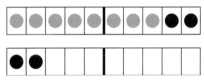

Moving two counters makes it easier to see that 8 + 4 = 12.

This week, your child will learn these new facts:

8 + 3 = 11	8 + 6 = 14
8 + 4 = 12	8 + 7 = 15
8 + 5 = 13	8 + 8 = 16

You will need:

- Ten-frames (page 57)
- Ten-frame cards 10–18 (page 53)
- 15 counters of two different colors (30 counters total)
- Two *Adding Eights* game boards (pages 71 and 73)
- Deck of cards, with ones, twos, tens, and face cards removed (28 cards total)
- Two game tokens
- Week 5 Practice Pages (pages 109–115)

DAY 1: NEW TEACHING

Warm-up activity

If your child has had any trouble recognizing the numbers in the teens on ten-frames, take a few moments to flash each ten-frame card for a second or two and ask how many boxes are full. Adjust your pace to your child, and stop and allow more time to look at a card if needed.

Introduce new facts

Write **8 + 4 =** on a piece of paper. Have your child help you model the problem with counters: Place eight counters of one color on the top ten-frame and four counters of another color on the bottom ten-frame.

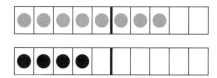

"To make it easier to figure out the answer, let's move two counters from the bottom row to the top row." Move two counters as shown.

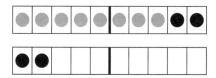

"How many counters are in the top row now?" *Ten.*
"How many counters are in the bottom row now?" *Two.*

"So, to solve eight plus four, you can add ten plus two instead. So, what's eight plus four?" *12.*

Have your child complete the written addition problem: **8 + 4 = 12**.

Repeat this process with the other +8 addition combinations that your child hasn't learned yet (8 + 3, 8 + 5, 8 + 6, 8 + 7, 8 + 8). Have your child physically move two counters from the bottom ten-frame to the top ten-frame each time to complete the row of ten and make each problem easier to solve.

Play *Adding Eights*

Teach your child how to play *Adding Eights* and play several times.

MATERIALS

- Two-page *Adding Eights* game board, edges trimmed and placed side by side to make one continuous game board (pages 71 and 73)

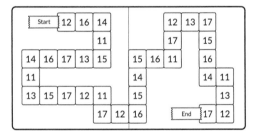

- Deck of cards, with ones, twos, tens, and face cards removed (28 cards total)
- Game token for each player

OBJECT OF THE GAME

Be the first player to reach the end of the game board.

HOW TO PLAY

Shuffle the cards and place them face down in a pile. Place each player's game token on Start.

To play, turn over the top card in the pile. Add eight to the number and then advance your token to the next space with that number. For example, if you turn over a six, advance your token to the next 14, since eight plus six equals 14. Play then passes to the other player. Continue until one of you reaches the end of the path.

As in previous weeks, allow your child to construct the numbers on the ten-frame if necessary, but encourage him to visualize the counters and figure out the answers mentally as his ability grows.

DAYS 2–5: ADDING EIGHTS AND PRACTICE PAGES

Each day, play *Adding Eights* several times. Then, have your child complete one Week 5 Practice Page. If he gets stuck, encourage him to visualize the numbers on the ten-frame or physically represent the numbers with counters.

Answers to this week's Practice Pages are on page 130.

WEEK 6

LOOK AT THE LEFTOVERS

WEEK 6 AT A GLANCE

Strategy: Look at the leftovers.

This week, your child will learn to solve the last few addition facts by combining fives to create a ten and then looking at the "leftovers." For example, to solve 7 + 6, your child will look for a group of five in each addend and combine the fives to make ten. Then, she'll add on the "leftover" counters. In this case, there are three additional counters, so 7 + 6 = 10 + 3, or 13.

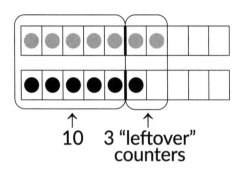

7 + 6 can be thought of as two groups of five, plus three "leftover" counters. So, 7 + 6 = 10 + 3, or 13.

This week, your child will learn these new facts:

6 + 5 = 11   7 + 5 = 12
6 + 6 = 12   7 + 6 = 13
7 + 4 = 11   7 + 7 = 14

You will need:

- Ten-frames (page 57)
- 15 counters of two different colors (30 counters total)
- Fives, sixes, sevens, eights, and nines from TWO decks of cards (40 cards total)
- Week 6 Practice Pages (pages 117–123)

DAY 1: NEW TEACHING

Introduce new facts

Write **7 + 6 =** on a piece of paper. Have your child help you model the problem with counters: Place seven counters of one color on the top ten-frame and six counters of another color on the bottom ten-frame.

Instead of moving any counters, ask your child to look for the group of five counters in each row.

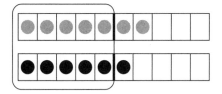

Point out that there are two groups of five. "How many counters are in the two groups of five?" *Ten.*

Then, point out the "leftover" counters: There are two counters left over in the top row and one counter left over in the bottom row.

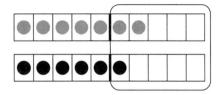

"How many counters are left over?" *Three.*

"To solve seven plus six, you can add ten plus three instead. So, what's seven plus six?" *13.*

Have your child complete the written addition problem: **7 + 6 = 13**.

Repeat this process for the other addition facts for this week. Each time, encourage your child to notice how many counters are left over after you put the two groups of five together.

For 7 + 4, encourage your child to imagine taking one counter from the seven and adding it to the row of four to make a five. Because there are now two groups of five, with one left over, the answer is 10 + 1, or 11.

Note

Some children prefer to solve these addition problems by making tens (as in weeks 4 and 5), rather than using the "look at the leftovers" strategy. That's fine! As long as your child has an efficient and reliable approach for solving these addition problems, she can use whichever approach makes the most sense to her.

Play *Addition War*

Teach your child how to play *Addition War* and play several times.

MATERIALS

- Fives, sixes, sevens, eights, and nines from TWO decks of cards (40 cards total)

OBJECT OF THE GAME

Win the most cards.

HOW TO PLAY

As in the regular card game War, shuffle the cards and deal out an equal number of cards to each player. Players place their cards face down in a pile.

To play, turn over the top two cards in your pile and announce their sum. For example, if you turn over a six and an eight, you would say, "Six plus eight equals 14." Then the other player turns over two cards and announces their sum. Whoever's sum is greater wins all four cards. If the sums are equal, play again. The player whose sum is greater wins all eight cards. Set aside the cards that are won.

Play until both players use up all the cards they were dealt. Whoever wins the most cards wins the game.

DAYS 2-5: ADDITION WAR AND PRACTICE PAGES

Each day, play *Addition War* several times. Then, have your child complete one Week 6 Practice Page to practice writing the answers to this week's addition facts and to review facts learned so far. If she gets stuck, encourage her to visualize the numbers on the ten-frame (or physically place counters on the ten-frame) and "look at the leftovers" to find the answers.

Answers to this week's Practice Pages are on page 95.

Congratulations!

Your child has now learned the strategies for all 81 addition facts! I hope you and your child have enjoyed the games and activities, and that you'll take some time to celebrate your child's accomplishment (and your own hard work, too)!

If your child has learned the strategies but cannot recall all of the facts automatically, continue playing the games and reinforcing the strategies as you play. It's also fine to simply go back through the entire book and review every strategy, if you find that your child doesn't have the addition facts down pat. Some children simply need a little more practice with the strategies before they know all the sums with ease. The addition facts are essential building blocks for success and confidence in math, so don't be afraid to spend as long as you need on them until they really stick for your child.

GAME BOARDS

Ten-frames

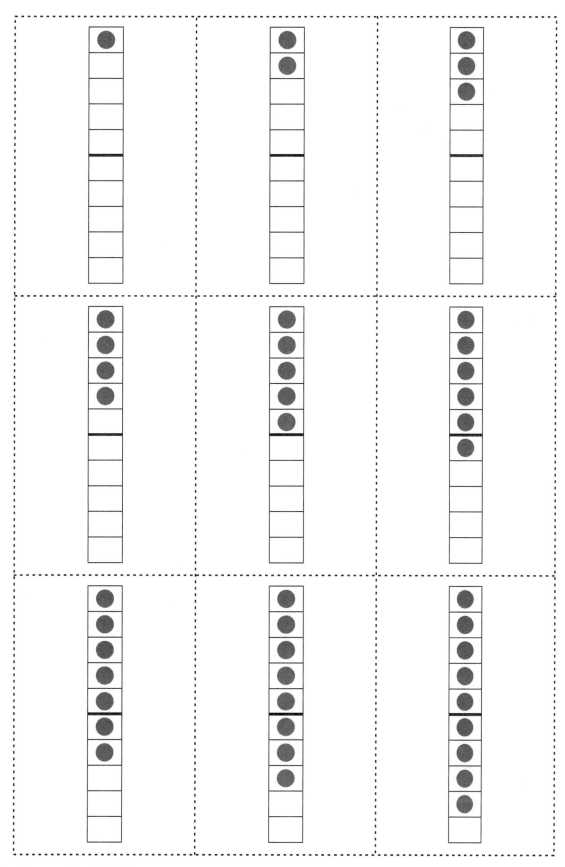

Ten-frame Cards 1-9

Climb to the Top

Climb to the Top

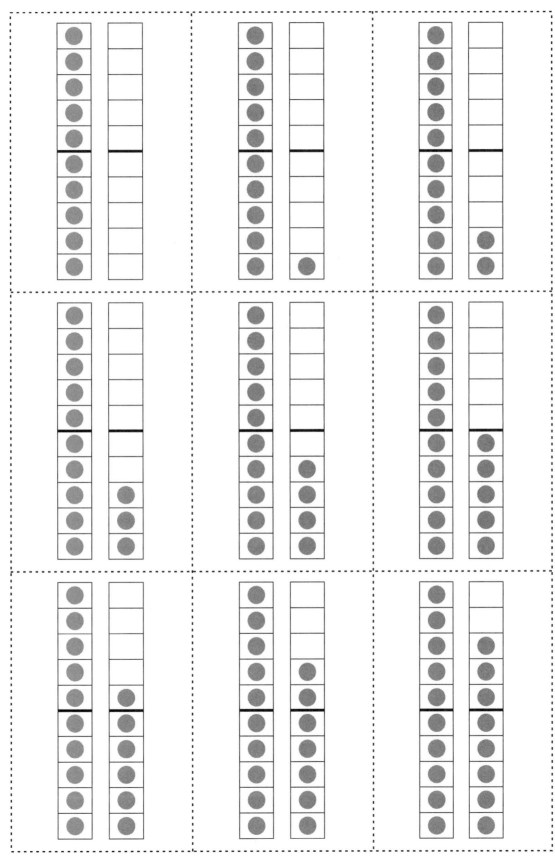

Ten-frame Cards 10-18

Adding Nines Bingo

16	12	15	13	18
17	18	13	14	12
13	14	FREE	12	15
15	11	16	10	14
10	13	11	16	17

Adding Nines Bingo

14	10	13	17	15
11	18	12	14	13
18	15	FREE	11	10
16	11	15	12	17
13	14	17	16	12

Adding

Start 12 16 14

11

14 16 17 13 15

11

13 15 17 12 11

17 12

Eights

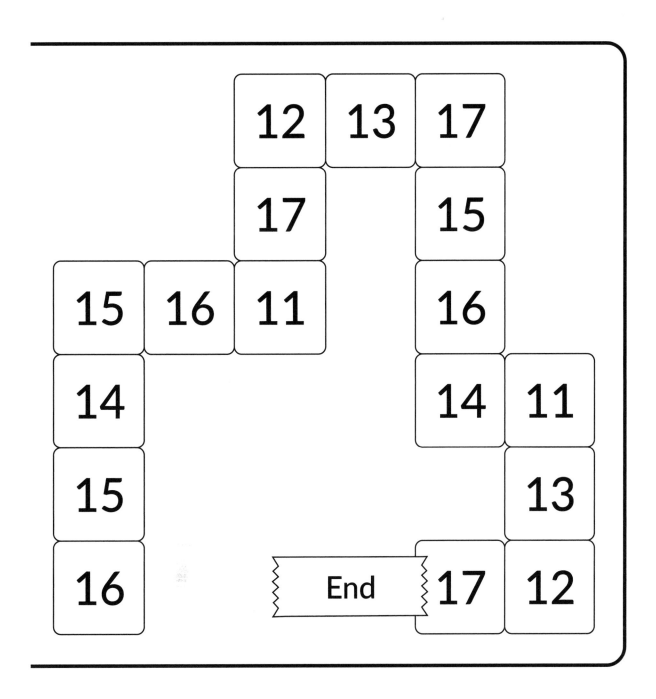

PRACTICE PAGES

Week 1: Adding One and Two   Practice Page 1

$1 + 2 =$ _____ $1 + 9 =$ _____ $1 + 7 =$ _____

$1 + 5 =$ _____ $4 + 2 =$ _____ $6 + 2 =$ _____

$7 + 2 =$ _____ $9 + 1 =$ _____ $2 + 2 =$ _____

$3 + 2 =$ _____ $1 + 1 =$ _____ $8 + 2 =$ _____

$1 + 8 =$ _____ $1 + 6 =$ _____ $1 + 4 =$ _____

$1 + 3 =$ _____ $1 + 2 =$ _____ $5 + 2 =$ _____

Week 1: Adding One and Two   **Practice Page 2**

$1 + 9 =$ _____ $1 + 2 =$ _____ $1 + 7 =$ _____

$4 + 2 =$ _____ $1 + 5 =$ _____ $6 + 2 =$ _____

$9 + 1 =$ _____ $7 + 2 =$ _____ $2 + 2 =$ _____

$1 + 1 =$ _____ $3 + 2 =$ _____ $8 + 2 =$ _____

$1 + 6 =$ _____ $1 + 8 =$ _____ $1 + 4 =$ _____

$1 + 2 =$ _____ $1 + 3 =$ _____ $5 + 2 =$ _____

Week 1: Adding One and Two   Practice Page 3

1 + 1 = _____   3 + 2 = _____   8 + 2 = _____

1 + 6 = _____   1 + 8 = _____   1 + 4 = _____

1 + 2 = _____   1 + 3 = _____   5 + 2 = _____

1 + 9 = _____   1 + 2 = _____   1 + 7 = _____

4 + 2 = _____   1 + 5 = _____   6 + 2 = _____

9 + 1 = _____   7 + 2 = _____   2 + 2 = _____

Week 1: Adding One and Two   **Practice Page 4**

$3 + 2 =$ _____ $8 + 2 =$ _____ $1 + 1 =$ _____

$1 + 8 =$ _____ $1 + 4 =$ _____ $1 + 6 =$ _____

$1 + 3 =$ _____ $5 + 2 =$ _____ $1 + 2 =$ _____

$1 + 2 =$ _____ $1 + 7 =$ _____ $1 + 9 =$ _____

$1 + 5 =$ _____ $6 + 2 =$ _____ $4 + 2 =$ _____

$7 + 2 =$ _____ $2 + 2 =$ _____ $9 + 1 =$ _____

Week 2: Pairs That Make Ten   ## Practice Page 1

$8 +$ _____ $= 10$ $9 +$ _____ $= 10$ $7 +$ _____ $= 10$

$6 +$ _____ $= 10$ $5 +$ _____ $= 10$ $4 +$ _____ $= 10$

$3 +$ _____ $= 10$ $1 +$ _____ $= 10$ $2 +$ _____ $= 10$

$3 + 2 =$ _____ $8 + 2 =$ _____ $1 + 1 =$ _____

$1 + 8 =$ _____ $1 + 4 =$ _____ $1 + 6 =$ _____

$1 + 3 =$ _____ $5 + 2 =$ _____ $1 + 2 =$ _____

Week 2: Pairs That Make Ten

Practice Page 2

$7 +$ _____ $= 10$ $5 +$ _____ $= 10$ $4 +$ _____ $= 10$

$9 +$ _____ $= 10$ $2 +$ _____ $= 10$ $3 +$ _____ $= 10$

$6 +$ _____ $= 10$ $1 +$ _____ $= 10$ $8 +$ _____ $= 10$

$1 + 9 =$ _____ $1 + 2 =$ _____ $1 + 7 =$ _____

$4 + 2 =$ _____ $1 + 5 =$ _____ $6 + 2 =$ _____

$8 + 2 =$ _____ $7 + 2 =$ _____ $2 + 2 =$ _____

Week 2: Pairs That Make Ten   Practice Page 3

6 + 4 = _____   3 + 2 = _____   8 + 2 = _____

1 + 6 = _____   1 + 8 = _____   1 + 4 = _____

1 + 2 = _____   5 + 5 = _____   5 + 2 = _____

1 + 9 = _____   1 + 2 = _____   4 + 6 = _____

7 + 3 = _____   1 + 5 = _____   6 + 2 = _____

4 + 2 = _____   7 + 2 = _____   3 + 7 = _____

Week 2: Pairs That Make Ten   Practice Page 4

$5 + 5 =$ _____ $8 + 2 =$ _____ $4 + 6 =$ _____

$1 + 8 =$ _____ $6 + 4 =$ _____ $1 + 6 =$ _____

$1 + 9 =$ _____ $5 + 2 =$ _____ $7 + 3 =$ _____

$2 + 8 =$ _____ $1 + 7 =$ _____ $9 + 1 =$ _____

$3 + 7 =$ _____ $6 + 2 =$ _____ $4 + 2 =$ _____

$7 + 2 =$ _____ $5 + 5 =$ _____ $5 + 2 =$ _____

Week 3: Sums Less Than Ten   ## Practice Page 1

$3 + 3 =$ _____ $5 + 5 =$ _____ $5 + 4 =$ _____

$9 + 1 =$ _____ $7 + 2 =$ _____ $3 + 5 =$ _____

$4 + 4 =$ _____ $2 + 8 =$ _____ $6 + 3 =$ _____

$3 + 4 =$ _____ $3 + 5 =$ _____ $4 + 4 =$ _____

$6 + 4 =$ _____ $3 + 3 =$ _____ $1 + 5 =$ _____

$2 + 4 =$ _____ $7 + 3 =$ _____ $4 + 3 =$ _____

$4 + 5 =$ _____ $6 + 2 =$ _____ $3 + 6 =$ _____

Week 3: Sums Less Than Ten   **Practice Page 2**

$5 + 4 =$ _____ $3 + 3 =$ _____ $1 + 9 =$ _____

$3 + 5 =$ _____ $3 + 7 =$ _____ $2 + 5 =$ _____

$6 + 3 =$ _____ $4 + 4 =$ _____ $8 + 1 =$ _____

$4 + 4 =$ _____ $3 + 4 =$ _____ $3 + 5 =$ _____

$8 + 2 =$ _____ $5 + 5 =$ _____ $3 + 3 =$ _____

$4 + 3 =$ _____ $1 + 6 =$ _____ $6 + 4 =$ _____

$3 + 6 =$ _____ $4 + 5 =$ _____ $7 + 1 =$ _____

Week 3: Sums Less Than Ten   Practice Page 3

$1 + 9 = $ _____ $5 + 4 = $ _____ $3 + 3 = $ _____

$2 + 5 = $ _____ $3 + 5 = $ _____ $3 + 7 = $ _____

$8 + 1 = $ _____ $6 + 3 = $ _____ $2 + 2 = $ _____

$1 + 1 = $ _____ $4 + 4 = $ _____ $3 + 2 = $ _____

$5 + 2 = $ _____ $8 + 2 = $ _____ $5 + 5 = $ _____

$6 + 4 = $ _____ $4 + 3 = $ _____ $1 + 6 = $ _____

$7 + 1 = $ _____ $3 + 6 = $ _____ $4 + 1 = $ _____

Week 3: Sums Less Than Ten

Practice Page 4

$5 + 5 =$ _____

$5 + 4 =$ _____

$4 + 2 =$ _____

$7 + 2 =$ _____

$3 + 5 =$ _____

$9 + 1 =$ _____

$2 + 8 =$ _____

$6 + 3 =$ _____

$4 + 4 =$ _____

$3 + 5 =$ _____

$4 + 4 =$ _____

$3 + 4 =$ _____

$1 + 3 =$ _____

$1 + 5 =$ _____

$6 + 4 =$ _____

$7 + 3 =$ _____

$4 + 3 =$ _____

$2 + 1 =$ _____

$6 + 2 =$ _____

$3 + 6 =$ _____

$4 + 5 =$ _____

Week 4: Adding Nine   ## Practice Page 1

$4 + 9 =$ _____ $9 + 2 =$ _____ $6 + 9 =$ _____

$9 + 1 =$ _____ $7 + 9 =$ _____ $3 + 9 =$ _____

$9 + 9 =$ _____ $9 + 8 =$ _____ $5 + 9 =$ _____

$3 + 6 =$ _____ $3 + 5 =$ _____ $4 + 4 =$ _____

$6 + 4 =$ _____ $3 + 3 =$ _____ $2 + 7 =$ _____

$3 + 1 =$ _____ $7 + 3 =$ _____ $5 + 5 =$ _____

$4 + 5 =$ _____ $6 + 2 =$ _____ $8 + 1 =$ _____

$2 + 2 =$ _____ $8 + 2 =$ _____ $4 + 3 =$ _____

Week 4: Adding Nine   Practice Page 2

$2 + 9 =$ _____ $9 + 6 =$ _____ $1 + 9 =$ _____

$9 + 7 =$ _____ $5 + 9 =$ _____ $4 + 9 =$ _____

$8 + 9 =$ _____ $9 + 3 =$ _____ $9 + 9 =$ _____

$4 + 5 =$ _____ $6 + 2 =$ _____ $2 + 3 =$ _____

$8 + 2 =$ _____ $5 + 1 =$ _____ $4 + 3 =$ _____

$1 + 6 =$ _____ $7 + 3 =$ _____ $5 + 5 =$ _____

$6 + 3 =$ _____ $3 + 3 =$ _____ $4 + 4 =$ _____

$4 + 6 =$ _____ $3 + 5 =$ _____ $2 + 7 =$ _____

Week 4: Adding Nine   **Practice Page 3**

$2 + 7 =$ _____ $1 + 9 =$ _____ $3 + 3 =$ _____

$5 + 9 =$ _____ $8 + 2 =$ _____ $9 + 7 =$ _____

$7 + 3 =$ _____ $1 + 2 =$ _____ $8 + 2 =$ _____

$3 + 5 =$ _____ $4 + 4 =$ _____ $4 + 5 =$ _____

$2 + 9 =$ _____ $6 + 9 =$ _____ $4 + 9 =$ _____

$9 + 3 =$ _____ $5 + 5 =$ _____ $5 + 2 =$ _____

$6 + 2 =$ _____ $9 + 9 =$ _____ $6 + 3 =$ _____

$8 + 9 =$ _____ $4 + 3 =$ _____ $4 + 6 =$ _____

Week 4: Adding Nine   Practice Page 4

$6 + 9 =$ _____ $4 + 9 =$ _____ $2 + 9 =$ _____

$5 + 5 =$ _____ $2 + 4 =$ _____ $9 + 3 =$ _____

$9 + 9 =$ _____ $6 + 3 =$ _____ $6 + 2 =$ _____

$4 + 3 =$ _____ $4 + 6 =$ _____ $8 + 9 =$ _____

$1 + 9 =$ _____ $3 + 3 =$ _____ $2 + 7 =$ _____

$8 + 2 =$ _____ $9 + 7 =$ _____ $5 + 9 =$ _____

$1 + 4 =$ _____ $8 + 2 =$ _____ $7 + 3 =$ _____

$4 + 4 =$ _____ $4 + 5 =$ _____ $3 + 5 =$ _____

Week 5: Adding Eight   Practice Page 1

4 + 8 = _____   8 + 2 = _____   6 + 8 = _____

8 + 1 = _____   7 + 8 = _____   3 + 8 = _____

8 + 9 = _____   8 + 8 = _____   5 + 8 = _____

3 + 6 = _____   3 + 5 = _____   4 + 4 = _____

6 + 4 = _____   3 + 3 = _____   2 + 7 = _____

9 + 7 = _____   7 + 3 = _____   5 + 5 = _____

4 + 5 = _____   6 + 2 = _____   8 + 9 = _____

6 + 9 = _____   9 + 4 = _____   4 + 3 = _____

Week 5: Adding Eight   **Practice Page 2**

2 + 8 = _____   8 + 6 = _____   1 + 8 = _____

8 + 7 = _____   5 + 8 = _____   4 + 8 = _____

8 + 8 = _____   8 + 3 = _____   8 + 9 = _____

4 + 5 = _____   6 + 2 = _____   9 + 6 = _____

9 + 9 = _____   3 + 9 = _____   4 + 3 = _____

1 + 6 = _____   7 + 3 = _____   5 + 5 = _____

6 + 3 = _____   5 + 9 = _____   4 + 4 = _____

4 + 6 = _____   3 + 5 = _____   2 + 7 = _____

Week 5: Adding Eight

Practice Page 3

$9 + 7 =$ _____

$1 + 8 =$ _____

$3 + 3 =$ _____

$5 + 8 =$ _____

$9 + 9 =$ _____

$8 + 7 =$ _____

$7 + 3 =$ _____

$1 + 2 =$ _____

$8 + 2 =$ _____

$3 + 5 =$ _____

$4 + 4 =$ _____

$4 + 5 =$ _____

$2 + 9 =$ _____

$6 + 8 =$ _____

$4 + 8 =$ _____

$8 + 3 =$ _____

$5 + 5 =$ _____

$5 + 9 =$ _____

$6 + 9 =$ _____

$8 + 9 =$ _____

$6 + 3 =$ _____

$8 + 8 =$ _____

$4 + 3 =$ _____

$4 + 6 =$ _____

Week 5: Adding Eight   **Practice Page 4**

$6 + 8 =$ _____ $4 + 8 =$ _____ $2 + 8 =$ _____

$5 + 5 =$ _____ $2 + 4 =$ _____ $8 + 3 =$ _____

$8 + 8 =$ _____ $6 + 3 =$ _____ $6 + 2 =$ _____

$4 + 3 =$ _____ $4 + 6 =$ _____ $8 + 9 =$ _____

$1 + 8 =$ _____ $9 + 3 =$ _____ $2 + 7 =$ _____

$8 + 2 =$ _____ $8 + 7 =$ _____ $5 + 8 =$ _____

$9 + 4 =$ _____ $9 + 7 =$ _____ $7 + 3 =$ _____

$4 + 4 =$ _____ $4 + 5 =$ _____ $6 + 9 =$ _____

Week 6: Look at the Leftovers   Practice Page 1

$6 + 5 =$ _____ $3 + 8 =$ _____ $4 + 3 =$ _____

$7 + 9 =$ _____ $5 + 5 =$ _____ $6 + 7 =$ _____

$8 + 6 =$ _____ $1 + 9 =$ _____ $9 + 4 =$ _____

$1 + 3 =$ _____ $6 + 6 =$ _____ $7 + 7 =$ _____

$6 + 3 =$ _____ $6 + 2 =$ _____ $5 + 9 =$ _____

$7 + 4 =$ _____ $3 + 2 =$ _____ $3 + 7 =$ _____

$2 + 2 =$ _____ $8 + 4 =$ _____ $7 + 5 =$ _____

$4 + 1 =$ _____ $5 + 4 =$ _____ $9 + 9 =$ _____

Week 6: Look at the Leftovers   Practice Page 2

7 + 7 = _____   5 + 1 = _____   8 + 5 = _____

3 + 5 = _____   9 + 6 = _____   2 + 8 = _____

2 + 9 = _____   7 + 6 = _____   8 + 8 = _____

9 + 3 = _____   5 + 2 = _____   6 + 6 = _____

5 + 6 = _____   3 + 3 = _____   4 + 6 = _____

6 + 1 = _____   4 + 2 = _____   4 + 7 = _____

7 + 8 = _____   5 + 7 = _____   7 + 2 = _____

4 + 4 = _____   7 + 1 = _____   8 + 9 = _____

Week 6: Look at the Leftovers   Practice Page 3

$3 + 8 =$ _____ $4 + 4 =$ _____ $7 + 4 =$ _____

$8 + 2 =$ _____ $3 + 9 =$ _____ $2 + 7 =$ _____

$6 + 5 =$ _____ $5 + 3 =$ _____ $9 + 6 =$ _____

$7 + 7 =$ _____ $5 + 1 =$ _____ $8 + 4 =$ _____

$3 + 3 =$ _____ $6 + 1 =$ _____ $6 + 6 =$ _____

$9 + 2 =$ _____ $7 + 6 =$ _____ $6 + 4 =$ _____

$7 + 1 =$ _____ $8 + 9 =$ _____ $5 + 2 =$ _____

$5 + 7 =$ _____ $4 + 2 =$ _____ $6 + 8 =$ _____

Week 6: Look at the Leftovers   Practice Page 4

$6 + 5 =$ _____ $5 + 4 =$ _____ $1 + 3 =$ _____

$1 + 9 =$ _____ $5 + 8 =$ _____ $7 + 4 =$ _____

$4 + 9 =$ _____ $3 + 6 =$ _____ $2 + 2 =$ _____

$4 + 1 =$ _____ $7 + 7 =$ _____ $5 + 9 =$ _____

$7 + 6 =$ _____ $8 + 8 =$ _____ $7 + 3 =$ _____

$4 + 3 =$ _____ $2 + 3 =$ _____ $7 + 9 =$ _____

$9 + 9 =$ _____ $5 + 7 =$ _____ $4 + 6 =$ _____

$6 + 2 =$ _____ $7 + 8 =$ _____ $6 + 6 =$ _____

ANSWER KEYS

Week 1: Adding One and Two		Practice Page 1
1 + 2 = 3	1 + 9 = 10	1 + 7 = 8
1 + 5 = 6	4 + 2 = 6	6 + 2 = 8
7 + 2 = 9	9 + 1 = 10	2 + 2 = 4
3 + 2 = 5	1 + 1 = 2	8 + 2 = 10
1 + 8 = 9	1 + 6 = 7	1 + 4 = 5
1 + 3 = 4	1 + 2 = 3	5 + 2 = 7

Week 1: Adding One and Two		Practice Page 2
1 + 9 = 10	1 + 2 = 3	1 + 7 = 8
4 + 2 = 6	1 + 5 = 6	6 + 2 = 8
9 + 1 = 10	7 + 2 = 9	2 + 2 = 4
1 + 1 = 2	3 + 2 = 5	8 + 2 = 10
1 + 6 = 7	1 + 8 = 9	1 + 4 = 5
1 + 2 = 3	1 + 3 = 4	5 + 2 = 7

Week 1: Adding One and Two		Practice Page 3
1 + 1 = 2	3 + 2 = 5	8 + 2 = 10
1 + 6 = 7	1 + 8 = 9	1 + 4 = 5
1 + 2 = 3	1 + 3 = 4	5 + 2 = 7
1 + 9 = 10	1 + 2 = 3	1 + 7 = 8
4 + 2 = 6	1 + 5 = 6	6 + 2 = 8
9 + 1 = 10	7 + 2 = 9	2 + 2 = 4

Week 1: Adding One and Two		Practice Page 4
3 + 2 = 5	8 + 2 = 10	1 + 1 = 2
1 + 8 = 9	1 + 4 = 5	1 + 6 = 7
1 + 3 = 4	5 + 2 = 7	1 + 2 = 3
1 + 2 = 3	1 + 7 = 8	1 + 9 = 10
1 + 5 = 6	6 + 2 = 8	4 + 2 = 6
7 + 2 = 9	2 + 2 = 4	9 + 1 = 10

Week 2: Pairs That Make Ten		Practice Page 1
8 + $\underline{2}$ = 10	9 + $\underline{1}$ = 10	7 + $\underline{3}$ = 10
6 + $\underline{4}$ = 10	5 + $\underline{5}$ = 10	4 + $\underline{6}$ = 10
3 + $\underline{7}$ = 10	1 + $\underline{9}$ = 10	2 + $\underline{8}$ = 10
3 + 2 = 5	8 + 2 = 10	1 + 1 = 2
1 + 8 = 9	1 + 4 = 5	1 + 6 = 7
1 + 3 = 4	5 + 2 = 7	1 + 2 = 3

Week 2: Pairs That Make Ten		Practice Page 2
7 + $\underline{3}$ = 10	5 + $\underline{5}$ = 10	4 + $\underline{6}$ = 10
9 + $\underline{1}$ = 10	2 + $\underline{8}$ = 10	3 + $\underline{7}$ = 10
6 + $\underline{4}$ = 10	1 + $\underline{9}$ = 10	8 + $\underline{2}$ = 10
1 + 9 = 10	1 + 2 = 3	1 + 7 = 8
4 + 2 = 6	1 + 5 = 6	6 + 2 = 8
8 + 2 = 10	7 + 2 = 9	2 + 2 = 4

Week 2: Pairs That Make Ten		Practice Page 3
6 + 4 = 10	3 + 2 = 5	8 + 2 = 10
1 + 6 = 7	1 + 8 = 9	1 + 4 = 5
1 + 2 = 3	5 + 5 = 10	5 + 2 = 7
1 + 9 = 10	1 + 2 = 3	4 + 6 = 10
7 + 3 = 10	1 + 5 = 6	6 + 2 = 8
4 + 2 = 6	7 + 2 = 9	3 + 7 = 10

Week 2: Pairs That Make Ten		Practice Page 4
5 + 5 = 10	8 + 2 = 10	4 + 6 = 10
1 + 8 = 9	6 + 4 = 10	1 + 6 = 7
1 + 9 = 10	5 + 2 = 7	7 + 3 = 10
2 + 8 = 10	1 + 7 = 8	9 + 1 = 10
3 + 7 = 10	6 + 2 = 8	4 + 2 = 6
7 + 2 = 9	5 + 5 = 10	5 + 2 = 7

Week 3: Sums Less Than Ten — Practice Page 1

3 + 3 = 6	5 + 5 = 10	5 + 4 = 9
9 + 1 = 10	7 + 2 = 9	3 + 5 = 8
4 + 4 = 8	2 + 8 = 10	6 + 3 = 9
3 + 4 = 7	3 + 5 = 8	4 + 4 = 8
6 + 4 = 10	3 + 3 = 6	1 + 5 = 6
2 + 4 = 6	7 + 3 = 10	4 + 3 = 7
4 + 5 = 9	6 + 2 = 8	3 + 6 = 9

Week 3: Sums Less Than Ten — Practice Page 2

5 + 4 = 9	3 + 3 = 6	1 + 9 = 10
3 + 5 = 8	3 + 7 = 10	2 + 5 = 7
6 + 3 = 9	4 + 4 = 8	8 + 1 = 9
4 + 4 = 8	3 + 4 = 7	3 + 5 = 8
8 + 2 = 10	5 + 5 = 10	3 + 3 = 6
4 + 3 = 7	1 + 6 = 7	6 + 4 = 10
3 + 6 = 9	4 + 5 = 9	7 + 1 = 8

Week 3: Sums Less Than Ten — Practice Page 3

1 + 9 = 10	5 + 4 = 9	3 + 3 = 6
2 + 5 = 7	3 + 5 = 8	3 + 7 = 10
8 + 1 = 9	6 + 3 = 9	2 + 2 = 4
1 + 1 = 2	4 + 4 = 8	3 + 2 = 5
5 + 2 = 7	8 + 2 = 10	5 + 5 = 10
6 + 4 = 10	4 + 3 = 7	1 + 6 = 7
7 + 1 = 8	3 + 6 = 9	4 + 1 = 5

Week 3: Sums Less Than Ten — Practice Page 4

5 + 5 = 10	5 + 4 = 9	4 + 2 = 6
7 + 2 = 9	3 + 5 = 8	9 + 1 = 10
2 + 8 = 10	6 + 3 = 9	4 + 4 = 8
3 + 5 = 8	4 + 4 = 8	3 + 4 = 7
1 + 3 = 4	1 + 5 = 6	6 + 4 = 10
7 + 3 = 10	4 + 3 = 7	2 + 1 = 3
6 + 2 = 8	3 + 6 = 9	4 + 5 = 9

Week 4: Adding Nine		Practice Page 1
4 + 9 = 13	9 + 2 = 11	6 + 9 = 15
9 + 1 = 10	7 + 9 = 16	3 + 9 = 12
9 + 9 = 18	9 + 8 = 17	5 + 9 = 14
3 + 6 = 9	3 + 5 = 8	4 + 4 = 8
6 + 4 = 10	3 + 3 = 6	2 + 7 = 9
3 + 1 = 4	7 + 3 = 10	5 + 5 = 10
4 + 5 = 9	6 + 2 = 8	8 + 1 = 9
2 + 2 = 4	8 + 2 = 10	4 + 3 = 7

Week 4: Adding Nine		Practice Page 2
2 + 9 = 11	9 + 6 = 15	1 + 9 = 10
9 + 7 = 16	5 + 9 = 14	4 + 9 = 13
8 + 9 = 17	9 + 3 = 12	9 + 9 = 18
4 + 5 = 9	6 + 2 = 8	2 + 3 = 5
8 + 2 = 10	5 + 1 = 6	4 + 3 = 7
1 + 6 = 7	7 + 3 = 10	5 + 5 = 10
6 + 3 = 9	3 + 3 = 6	4 + 4 = 8
4 + 6 = 10	3 + 5 = 8	2 + 7 = 9

Week 4: Adding Nine		Practice Page 3
2 + 7 = 9	1 + 9 = 10	3 + 3 = 6
5 + 9 = 14	8 + 2 = 10	9 + 7 = 16
7 + 3 = 10	1 + 2 = 3	8 + 2 = 10
3 + 5 = 8	4 + 4 = 8	4 + 5 = 9
2 + 9 = 11	6 + 9 = 15	4 + 9 = 13
9 + 3 = 12	5 + 5 = 10	5 + 2 = 7
6 + 2 = 8	9 + 9 = 18	6 + 3 = 9
8 + 9 = 17	4 + 3 = 7	4 + 6 = 10

Week 4: Adding Nine		Practice Page 4
6 + 9 = 15	4 + 9 = 13	2 + 9 = 11
5 + 5 = 10	2 + 4 = 6	9 + 3 = 12
9 + 9 = 18	6 + 3 = 9	6 + 2 = 8
4 + 3 = 7	4 + 6 = 10	8 + 9 = 17
1 + 9 = 10	3 + 3 = 6	2 + 7 = 9
8 + 2 = 10	9 + 7 = 16	5 + 9 = 14
1 + 4 = 5	8 + 2 = 10	7 + 3 = 10
4 + 4 = 8	4 + 5 = 9	3 + 5 = 8

Week 5: Adding Eight		Practice Page 1
4 + 8 = 12	8 + 2 = 10	6 + 8 = 14
8 + 1 = 9	7 + 8 = 15	3 + 8 = 11
8 + 9 = 17	8 + 8 = 16	5 + 8 = 13
3 + 6 = 9	3 + 5 = 8	4 + 4 = 8
6 + 4 = 10	3 + 3 = 6	2 + 7 = 9
9 + 7 = 16	7 + 3 = 10	5 + 5 = 10
4 + 5 = 9	6 + 2 = 8	8 + 9 = 17
6 + 9 = 15	9 + 4 = 13	4 + 3 = 7

Week 5: Adding Eight		Practice Page 2
2 + 8 = 10	8 + 6 = 14	1 + 8 = 9
8 + 7 = 15	5 + 8 = 13	4 + 8 = 12
8 + 8 = 16	8 + 3 = 11	8 + 9 = 17
4 + 5 = 9	6 + 2 = 8	9 + 6 = 15
9 + 9 = 18	3 + 9 = 12	4 + 3 = 7
1 + 6 = 7	7 + 3 = 10	5 + 5 = 10
6 + 3 = 9	5 + 9 = 14	4 + 4 = 8
4 + 6 = 10	3 + 5 = 8	2 + 7 = 9

Week 5: Adding Eight		Practice Page 3
9 + 7 = 16	1 + 8 = 9	3 + 3 = 6
5 + 8 = 13	9 + 9 = 18	8 + 7 = 15
7 + 3 = 10	1 + 2 = 3	8 + 2 = 10
3 + 5 = 8	4 + 4 = 8	4 + 5 = 9
2 + 9 = 11	6 + 8 = 14	4 + 8 = 12
8 + 3 = 11	5 + 5 = 10	5 + 9 = 14
6 + 9 = 15	8 + 9 = 17	6 + 3 = 9
8 + 8 = 16	4 + 3 = 7	4 + 6 = 10

Week 5: Adding Eight		Practice Page 4
6 + 8 = 14	4 + 8 = 12	2 + 8 = 10
5 + 5 = 10	2 + 4 = 6	8 + 3 = 11
8 + 8 = 16	6 + 3 = 9	6 + 2 = 8
4 + 3 = 7	4 + 6 = 10	8 + 9 = 17
1 + 8 = 9	9 + 3 = 12	2 + 7 = 9
8 + 2 = 10	8 + 7 = 15	5 + 8 = 13
9 + 4 = 13	9 + 7 = 16	7 + 3 = 10
4 + 4 = 8	4 + 5 = 9	6 + 9 = 15

Week 6: Look at the Leftovers		Practice Page 1
6 + 5 = 11	3 + 8 = 11	4 + 3 = 7
7 + 9 = 16	5 + 5 = 10	6 + 7 = 13
8 + 6 = 14	1 + 9 = 10	9 + 4 = 13
1 + 3 = 4	6 + 6 = 12	7 + 7 = 14
6 + 3 = 9	6 + 2 = 8	5 + 9 = 14
7 + 4 = 11	3 + 2 = 5	3 + 7 = 10
2 + 2 = 4	8 + 4 = 12	7 + 5 = 12
4 + 1 = 5	5 + 4 = 9	9 + 9 = 18

Week 6: Look at the Leftovers		Practice Page 2
7 + 7 = 14	5 + 1 = 6	8 + 5 = 13
3 + 5 = 8	9 + 6 = 15	2 + 8 = 10
2 + 9 = 11	7 + 6 = 13	8 + 8 = 16
9 + 3 = 12	5 + 2 = 7	6 + 6 = 12
5 + 6 = 11	3 + 3 = 6	4 + 6 = 10
6 + 1 = 7	4 + 2 = 6	4 + 7 = 11
7 + 8 = 15	5 + 7 = 12	7 + 2 = 9
4 + 4 = 8	7 + 1 = 8	8 + 9 = 17

Week 6: Look at the Leftovers		Practice Page 3
3 + 8 = 11	4 + 4 = 8	7 + 4 = 11
8 + 2 = 10	3 + 9 = 12	2 + 7 = 9
6 + 5 = 11	5 + 3 = 8	9 + 6 = 15
7 + 7 = 14	5 + 1 = 6	8 + 4 = 12
3 + 3 = 6	6 + 1 = 7	6 + 6 = 12
9 + 2 = 11	7 + 6 = 13	6 + 4 = 10
7 + 1 = 8	8 + 9 = 17	5 + 2 = 7
5 + 7 = 12	4 + 2 = 6	6 + 8 = 14

Week 6: Look at the Leftovers		Practice Page 4
6 + 5 = 11	5 + 4 = 9	1 + 3 = 4
1 + 9 = 10	5 + 8 = 13	7 + 4 = 11
4 + 9 = 13	3 + 6 = 9	2 + 2 = 4
4 + 1 = 5	7 + 7 = 14	5 + 9 = 14
7 + 6 = 13	8 + 8 = 16	7 + 3 = 10
4 + 3 = 7	2 + 3 = 5	7 + 9 = 16
9 + 9 = 18	5 + 7 = 12	4 + 6 = 10
6 + 2 = 8	7 + 8 = 15	6 + 6 = 12